PRAISE FOR

FLYING ON INVISIBLE WINGS

The poet invites us to share his journey to a world
where bodies are celebrated and souls mingle
in song. Garmendía's world is a place where
poems create new lands, and magic rules.

KIM DRAMER, PH.D.
Author and art historian

A life intensively lived, an endless stream of
emotional states, melancholic wanderings
of the acute consciousness owned by Félix.
He becomes the poem of our lives.
He transforms extremes into magic.
An immense task accomplished by
an immense heart.

ROSABEL OTÓN OLIVIERI
*Actress, director, professor of theater studies
at the University of Puerto Rico since 2000*

A poet owns his soul, a poet never dies,
the poem is alive in trees, dancing in the wind,
flying like a bird, a poet is free from suffering,
a poet lives in the beauty of life's soul,
enters its divine home and feels the timeless pleasure
that pervades everything.

We have in Félix a great poet, the man that struggles
to endure in beauty, the wise soul that seeks the
essence of life: the philosopher, the lover, his friend.

NELLY JO CARMONA
Actress and writer

A radiantly unique poetic voice.
Félix blends both imagination and somber reality
as he discusses the places he's lived and visited,
and people he's known. The wonderland
of Félix's poetic world is alive and well in these pages.

FRANNIE ZELLMAN, M.A. creative writing
Editor and contributor to the **Fat Poets Speak** *series*

To say Félix Garmendía has a way with words
doesn't begin to give his writing here justice.
His words are an entry point into a life well lived,
but a challenged life, too. Felix spares nothing;
his emotions are laid bare in the most extraordinarily
touching and accessible way. Sharing his remarkable
journey via his poetry conveys a gift
that we must all learn from.

BOB LEAHY
Publisher, PositiveLite.com

Menéalo, Menéalo, de aquí pallá, de allá pacá.
Menéalo, que se empelota.
Stir it, stir it around and around or it will curdle…
Those were the playful lyrics to the dance
of many tiny crabs that tickled the world's belly
and allowed for the birth of the Island of Puerto Rico.
Félix Garmendía was the narrator of the mythic story
that traveled from town to town and from square to
square delighting audiences some forty years ago.
Through his journey Félix has been fine tuning the
art of storytelling, listening, dancing,
and writing meaningful poetry so that life
will never stand still.
Menéalo.

ROSA LUISA MÁRQUEZ
Professor at University of Puerto Rico 1978–2011
with a specialty in Latin American contemporary theater.
Director, playwright, actress

FLYING ON INVISIBLE WINGS

FÉLIX GARMENDÍA

PEARLSONG PRESS
NASHVILLE, TN

Pearlsong Press
P.O. Box 58065
Nashville, TN 37205
http://www.pearlsong.com
http://www.pearlsongpress.com

Original trade paperback ISBN: 978-1-59719-093-0
Ebook ISBN: 978-1-59719-094-7

The story of Bela/Bella first appeared in PositiveLite.com
May 2016.

    Library of Congress Cataloging-in-Publication Data

Names: Garmendía, Félix, 1961–author.
Title: Flying on invisible wings / Félix Garmendía.
Description: Nashville, TN : Pearlsong Press, [2019]
Identifiers: LCCN 2019018200 (print) | LCCN
2019018929 (ebook) | ISBN
   9781597190947 (ebook) | ISBN 9781597190930 (trade
pbk. : alk. paper)
Classification: LCC PS3607.A755 (ebook) | LCC PS3607.
A755 A6 2019 (print) |
   DDC 811/.6—dc23
LC record available at https://lccn.loc.gov/2019018200

To my husband, Denis Beale,
the poem I live.

INTRODUCTION

"The whole is more than the sum of the parts."

Felix and I are not just a "couple" or "boyfriends." Felix and I are a family. As an avid member of Ancestry.com, I glory in the notion that future family tree detectives who stumble across us there will know we were married. We're just as married as JFK and Jackie, George and Martha Washington, Queen Elizabeth and Prince Phillip.

As a family we tackle what life throws at us together, and so far, it looks like we've been pretty good at it—we're still here. We have both been embedded in the history of the worldwide AIDS crisis since its beginning in the early '80s, our combined duration being over 60 years. We both know that life is a gift and waking up every day is a victory that should be celebrated, and that is and has been our goal. We celebrate life together.

Being around while Felix creates his paintings using words is a joy. Some are pastels, some watercolors, some oil paintings, yet others crayon drawings and sometimes even finger paintings. Art is awesome. Sitting 6 feet away from the artist busy creating, always ready to supply sufficient amounts of *arroz con pollo*, is even MORE awesome and gratifying for me.

DENIS BEALE

Wind and water change the land. Under im-mense pressure the diamond is born in the entrails of the Earth. There are pieces of shattered unicorns, playful gargoyles and frozen roses from the effect of life recorded in every one of these poems. A tale of resilience that carved these pieces of my life in words of stone. Each and every one is either a fraction of a shattered mirror or the punch of light coming out of the collision. It is the life story of a man that lives intensely, dancing on the edge of a blade, living by burning his candle from both ends.

These poems contain the names of those gone by and the lessons learned by their presence in my life, the tribute to those who left a trail of fireflies in my darkest nights. They contain the experiences of my years growing up in Puerto Rico to life in New York, New York and the deep exploration of my homo-sexual identity, the result of 21 years hiding and the liberating happiness of coming out in 1982. Then comes the beginning of the dark ages of AIDS and the death sentence received in 1989.

Among these poems there are fossilized footprints

of old loves, the struggles with IBM (Inclusion Body Myositis), and my journey since I landed in a wheelchair in 2013. These poems are a route in the map of finding the deepest human connection in my life: my partner, Denis. He is the rainbow flag that marks "home," the 21-year-old star smile embrace after 21 years of hiding, and my husband of six years by the law of the land.

In 1969 I was 8 years old, two years before I visited New York City for the first time. I was unaware of my reality when "the Stonewall Riots" in Greenwich Village, downtown Manhattan, were marking the beginning of LGBT rights. This year at the end of June New York City dresses in rainbow colors to celebrate the 50th anniversary of the beginning of the fight for LGBT human rights.

This book is an insight of a life lived without fear—or maybe the result of being terrified and taking a leap of hope. I type now with one hand, as my muscles shut down. This book tells the story of my lust for living even in a wheelchair, but with the seed of optimism as long as I can keep writing.

FÉLIX GARMENDÍA
February 2, 2019

CONTENTS

I
FAMILY
AND
YOUNGER
DAYS

We cover our children's eyes when we think it's too early in their lives for them to see the "light." It was done to me, and by the time I opened my eyes it was dark and much more difficult to find my way.

FG

Edna

Your own mom left early.
You called grandma *titi*. (Spanish for auntie).
My mom called you sister.
Devoted as a Capistrano swallow
to grandma,
and a respected teacher, like grandma,
mother of two girls, you later divorced.
Every afternoon you drank Coca-Cola with grandma,
I sat and listened, comforted:
the touch and words of mothers, more consistent
than those of an inconsistent god,
lavender perfume softening the air.
You taught me to play the guitar, scolded my temper,
grew my love for old things:
old lanterns,
coins.
You taught me to build sea landscapes:
driftwood, dried sea urchins, shells, dreams
in night lights, ocean waves.
We preserved flowers between wells of words,
putting them to sleep in books,
decorated picture frames.
As you taught me to preserve the past,
you learned my secret,
and you managed to put together
the once broken child,
as you would a faded doll.
In your footsteps, I met
and loved Venice

and its old glass.

You were also mom's shoulder to rest sadness on
when life seemed to close in on her.

I moved to New York. You went to Florida.
I heard your voice on the phone.

When you left, part of mom went with you
and part of me held you one more time,
made whole again,
like me, like the doll,
in my dreams.

Take Me Back

Light in the dark time,
sunrise in my days,
youngest brother.
I, the oldest.
With doubts that you vanquished
as you liberated my closet,
greeted me as I opened,
blossoming in pride.

I remember your yellow-green eyes,
your jokes.
You were like a grown-up child.
Your happiness bubbled.
Your loyalty was a soft melody
when my peace was disturbed.
How your grin comforted me.
Tiger cub, who would play
with speed and danger.

I moved away;
your light dimmed.
Alpha and Omega severed in Pangea.
Separated by the limits of land.
Separated by ocean and shivered,
like the bubble that lands on freshly mowed grass.

Then one day
when I hoped to see you,
you left abruptly.

Félix Garmendía   *17*

Doing what you loved,
speeding in excitement,
your life stopped.

These days I am old,
sick.
Losing myself at times
in the darkness of your absence.
Like the old Japanese art of restoring the ruptured,
my splintered bleeding kintsugi heart
needs to be repaired, with the old craft
of gold on your smile.
I can't leave just yet.
It's still not my time.
But these days,
I repair with the gold of memory
your tiger eyes
in my broken days,
my interrupted smile.

The mere echo of the beat
of your heart next to mine
holds me to life.
At times, I fake a smile
and pretend.
I will keep on living,
as long as you promise,
on my darkest night,
to show up in my sleep,
roar gently
and rip me from this earth
to get me back to you.

GRANDMA'S ROSES

Grandma gardened, tended fruit trees: mango, guava,
    sugar apple,
cantaloupes.
Her dogs adored her.
So did the school kids she taught.
She drove when women didn't.
Raised three children herself.
In 1984,
when I brought hand blown glass vases
from Venice,
She showed me three roses.
"See this closed rosebud? That is your little sister,
she is just a promise at this point."
Pointing out at an almost fully opened rose: "That is
    your mother."
Looking at the third rose she, pointed at herself.
This rose was losing its petals.
"I'm this rose. I used to be a shy bud.
I fell in love with grandpa, the sun opening my petals.
Like my garden,
I bloomed with fragrant colors.
Time passed, I grew after the trimming of my
    branches.
After years
my rose bowed her head, her crown fell.
I am the faded color rose, but I carry the seed.
The circle of life succeeds.
You will see new roses soon."

Grandma left May 11th 1993, but the rose lesson
      stayed.
Today the dusty Murano glass vases hold dried baby's
      breath
from our wedding boutonnieres, my husband's and
      mine.
The circle of life succeeds:

Grandma
Mom
Sister
Husband

The garden continues.

IN SEARCH OF MEANING

I started early in life,
looking at rocks and leaf skeletons
that I found while looking down.
I was tangled up in time
and dreams of growing up.
Defeated
way too early.
Too much time with tired, droopy eyelids from
        crying.
As time went by, I learned to sit up.
Then I managed to stand up
and I used my arms to squeeze
the nurturing cloud milk needed for my growth.
Then and there, my eyes level with life,
I found the living green leaves and the shining stars
that occasionally threw rocks at my sleepy planet.

Today, I'm getting to that age
where most survivors start weaving blankets
with the webs of past pain.

FÉLIX GARMENDÍA   *21*

Stardust (Mom)

Very much anticipated,
I was her firstborn.
She, the queen of my younger days.
The first one to protect me
against intolerance.
A fighter for independence
strong
bright as stardust,
drawing rainbow verses
on my skies.

Later on
life became life,
when one of us was taken too soon.
Something deep inside fractured her;
her nights threw shadows over her daylights.
After more than a decade, she still
hums the sadness
of my brother Kurt's death,
smiles these days are rare,
her skin delicate.
She is thin, like the explanation
given by god to mortals
about becoming old.
And the weight of ages
falls on her tired shoulders.
Like a thirsty cut rose.
Her beauty never left
but the nights became eternal

and she sat in a dark corner,
going through memories,
looking at photos of those gone.
A clock
that forgets to chime.
Or a book on a forgotten shelf.

How wish I could heal the grey shadows in your eyes:
my brother's death
my father's sudden absence
my departure to New York
the interrupted melody
of once a joyful song.
Mom
living tangled up between
shades of blue
deafened horns
her hopes an undelivered prayer,
to a sleepy god.
Mom,
like a soft whisper
of past winters.
Still trying to sing her interrupted song.

Roxana, Mi Hermana

Ten years after my birth, you landed tenderly on my
      lap.
I remember mom bringing you from the hospital.
She said, "they smile like angels when they sleep
as if they can fly."
First girl after four boys, the most precious present
      from the universe.
An April girl, diamond among us,
grace, your funny demeanor, laughter.
the queen of the hive.
Dad's little girl, adored, protected, the darkness of a
      musical night teaching the stars to sing.
Strong, talented, independent.
The alpha and the omega of the Garmendía family,
      linked forever, keeping the chain strong
as you insisted that we all keep talking
through arguments and fights.

When one of us departed, a part of all of us died.
We held our hands together and with the strength of
      one, we faced the storm.

I was next to you when your first attempt at love
      failed
and we both cried and hugged, finding comfort.
We said "see you soon" when I came to New York,
the words of our hearts drowning,
stuck in our throats.

Time passed.

You married.
You settled in a house not far
From our mom.
Your life is far from easy,
but very much anchored in commitment,
ballerina now mother earth in hope.
You've danced with your children
through their days
and years.
Your harvest: their grins
and their strength
much like your own.
Much like what you give
to us still.

Mi hermana.
My sister.

MUSIC

Looking at a statue of Pan teaching the flute to a
      young man, in my living room,
made me think of how music nested in my treetops,
rain of silences that exploded in musical notes when
      they hit the ground.
My childhood staff was sprinkled with unexpected
      sounds,
from my father's tangos to my mother's Ukrainian
      tunes. None of them at all Puerto Rican.
Favorites were repeated, "Mona Lisa" and others by
      Nat King Cole.
Opera was a constant part of the background music,
      maybe the reason I dislike it so much.
I can take an aria here and there but the three hours
      plus of *The Valkyrie* left me comatose.
I come from a land where music flows in our veins.
Spanish, Indian and the fire of African drums
melted the lifecycle of a proud Caribbean cultural
      identity.
At an early age, I was introduced to ballads;
sad songs seemed to fit my profile.
I remember listening to 45s late at night on my
      yellow turntable.
Dionne Warwick, Bee Gees, Barry Manilow, Barbra,
      and our beloved Puerto Rican singer Glenn
      Monroig.
I received communion from the romance of their
      voices.
I related to my blues and rejected, in life and out, any

happy tune.
Rock and roll was too happy for me.
And tangled up in sadness I embraced the blues.
Happy music was in exile.
And from those somber melodies,
I early developed a bleak sense of life.
Until one day I fell in love and found my
happy tunes woke up.
Elton John, Sylvester, Gloria Gaynor, and the magic
era of disco taught me to dance.
I felt happy.
It was loneliness that colored my sounds in tones of
grey and black.
I became one with love and my music taste expanded.
In the '80s I found the soundtrack of my early life.
And danced till exhaustion, until my wings were
begging to fly.
Music, the time machine that brings us back and
forth into a dream of profound sadness or
immense bliss.
In 1990 Madonna confronted the establishment,
introducing Vogue and bringing up to light an
underground culture of gay New York.
She kissed saints, burned crosses, in general she pissed
off the church.
Madonna became my idol, the voice of the oppressed.
Then came the millennium and my younger years
started to fade;
music became repetitive, tired angry and violent.

I was slowing down and becoming old.
And I started backing up from it.
I guess it becomes the complaint of most of us.
The good old days felt better.
But I must say, music has power;
it makes the palm play with the wind.
When hot ember notes consume each other in a kiss.
Pressure of life and feelings turn charcoal into
            diamonds,
making us remember one thing,
music is the background of our lives.
We get to choose the tune to dance to.

Papi

He seems made of granite.
My father,
stone image in which lines have been etched
by decades of growth and change.
We spoke little for a while,
but we came together again
spring after winter
adult child and man.
From stone and glass
under my toes
he became the rock of an anchor.

When I was strong, he was absent.
Somewhere lost in between loves
he chased.
But at the moment I needed him,
when I fell sick, he became my refuge.

I am deteriorating fast
but he gives my sick body
a comfortable shadow:
tree's roots, strong trunk, soft jade leaves.

I might breach the script
and leave this earth before him.
Life brands another norm
on the younger
when we depart our older ones.
But I'll take with me his strength

Félix Garmendía

his old oak intense ways,
his titan touch.

I have found the right time to forgive
the early bumpy road
and now fall in love with him
leaving this planet singing
a song he taught me.

I will hum,
riding a comet and feeling complete.

THE GREETING

I was very young, so young that I thought I was alone.
He showed up on a summer afternoon.
I remember the night when we silently watched stars
      under the Puerto Rican sky.

Electricity.
The first time I saw him, my spine froze.
He was a bird about to break free,
or a pulsating cocoon expecting the birth of wings.
—"Hi, my name is Felix."
—"Nice to meet you, I'm Pablo."

The singer, the actor, the rosebud.
I was closer to the sun of my truth.
My light blinded him with the fear of my touch.

...And we started to weave dreams and hopes.
I was new at the game, but full of life and lust.
Young but aware.
He was a small blue fire, but he would have put
      Hephaestus to shame.

It was his idea, "the Vulcan greeting." He had to
      explain it to me.
From that day on, we saluted each other.
The summer went by...
A short flame, a small candle that died with his fears
      of facing himself.

FÉLIX GARMENDÍA

Then the goodbye when I went back to college, our
        tears close to a kiss.

Away from him, I found my place under the sun and
        woke to myself
in the middle of a storm of lust.

He still sings. I hear his echoes tangled up in my
        dreams.

Today, I remember you, Pablo.
Leonard Nimoy, your Vulcan deity, passed away.
Before he departed this earth, he remembered our
        quiet spark under that night full of stars.
And left a message
for the tiny flame our young years couldn't keep.

I hope these days that you burn rabidly, that your
        veins are awakened to the pulsating chest of
        another man.

I salute your physical absence. Live long and prosper.

THE HOUR GLASS

After two decades of denial, I broke the hour glass.
Until 22, not even a kiss. I admired hairy chests from
        afar: looking up to a tall Spruce.
Arms like tree limbs, the raw shoulders.
Strong handshakes on my little hand.
A voice the chord of a father in my young mind.
Glistening silver backs with sweaty hairs under the
        Puerto Rican sun.
As early as 7, I imagined.

In the summer of 1982, some urge crawled out of my
        skin, a long-muted scream.
A hungry bat awakened from hibernation, looking
        for something to devour.
A warm red aura refracted in the flames
for the touch of another man.
Famine in front of the cauldron of lust.
No time to waste, my decision was made.
Fear wrestled desire on my throat.

An XXX theater in San Juan, famous for the queer
        action on the second floor.
A stranger.
The pleasure I denied myself for so long.
On my knees, I knelt, but not to the plaster god.
I swallowed the wood of a stranger after waiting for
        years.
That balmy afternoon, many things fell in place.

I gladly embraced the snake, not the old white lie.
Forever sex, not tales of anger from the clouds.
Forever hunger life yearning god of lust.

II
FROM
PUERTO RICO
TO NEW YORK

When entering the secret land of another being, don't invade like a conquistador. Plant a field of forget-me-nots to decorate your presence in their land.

FG

FROM PUERTO RICO
TO NEW YORK

I was born in paradise
cushioned by blue open skies
timid mountains covered in rainbows of impatiens
      and maidenhair ferns.
Where the sea hugs the ocean for 100 miles
to fresh air and passion fruit from my Ponce home
      to San Juan.

Puerto Rico is an infant island,
foster child of a rain forest of simple dichotomies of
      good and bad.
In its soul, Puerto Rico carries the force of a furious
      hurricane
and a smiling deity covered with the persistent
      melody of the coquí.
Therein lies the greatness of our blood
painted with sleepy innocence on the canvas of a
      green foliage smiling semi god.
Where the growth of my people
has been knifed by others for too long.
Our food, the nectar of the orchids.
Our music, an unfinished torch song of blessings
mixed with Taino, Spanish and African blood,
three grains of wood of our collective keel.
We carved a thousand saints from that wood.
A million rhymes with the heartbeat of a conga drum.
And the lullaby-hymn that we all murmured to each
      other when the night falls over the land.

We have been owned.
We have been a prize of a war contest
that Spain refunded from its treasure chest.
But the beauty of our people pervades,
still lightens up the morning sun.
Puerto Rico has been bound for centuries
over the iron chests of chronic conquistadors.
But we wake up every day, believing in the greatness
        of our mahogany race.
Even though for many of us,
Puerto Rico hurts like an open wound.

For there was no place for my love for men,
my place in your tribe.

So, twenty seven years ago,
with broken wings and eager soul,
I arrived in New York.
A promised land covered by snow.
Winter of 1988.
I had not loved for seven years.

Three decades after,
I find myself accomplished in the force of love.
Man to man embrace made law by the north.

And I withhold a tiny tear,
as the dreams arrive,
the warmest of your gods,
to keep my absence unnoticed.

I will not see you again.

THANK YOU, NUEVA YORK

In the winter of 1988
I left Puerto Rico behind,
a half-lived life,
not appreciated.
New York City
loved me and I loved it.
No darkness or shame
that people threw at me in Puerto Rico:
ordered to walk behind.
Shamed for walking by their side.
My hand held
to make sure I knew my place,
I, kneeling and quiet.
A slave to the beat of a dying heart.

New York City was Spring.
I became flower and hummingbird.
I decorated my body.
I was forbidden fruit:
Sex, love, drugs, pleasures of the flesh,
thorn and rose crowned my nights.
I was loved,
not received with a noose of shame.
This city gave me wings, my right to fly.
Thirty years in New York City,
loved for sure three times,
I have sown seeds with many men.
I found my lost child here,
my own man.

FÉLIX GARMENDÍA   *39*

When at last I do leave,
The wind will scatter me everywhere:
Central Park, Washington Heights, Hudson and East
        River, Upper West Side, Saint John the
        Divine Cathedral.

And from my thankful ashes, a tree will bloom.

GARGOYLES

Carrying the dust of ages, they watch us from afar.
Eyes open, dried cracked stone skin.
Stoic presences that guard us from the heights where
     they nest.
Fossils of forgotten chivalry.
Rock winged creatures that forgot how to fly.
They are the gargoyles of New York City,
the last survivors of centuries gone by.
They arrived in America under the crowded slave
     boats.
They hid in Puritan Bibles and lurked around
     treetops in New Amsterdam nights.
Their jaguar teeth, their vulture claws, were ready to
     capture and devour the unaware.
They needed to satisfy their ages old hunger.
During the '90s I became a hunter of men and
     gargoyles.
They both fascinated me.
Their strength
Their lust
The endangered will to live intensely, caught between
     our need to breed and the stone cold fear of
     HIV/AIDS.
I remember those steamy nights, where you can hear
     from lust the beats of your own heart.
And I went ahead like many times before, in search
     of gargoyles.
I jumped in the subway, armed with a lighter and a
     few joints.

Not having an idea where to go.
I would ride the subway until I heard a siren cry.
It was my cue to start my search.
I left the train and smoked a "J."
My eyes were looking for gargoyles, the ones that return
        the favor by looking right back at me.
Eye to eye.
Sometimes I found a new one; most of the time I said
        hello to old stone friends.
It was the thrill of the hunting, the fuel of the joint,
        and the finding of the new one.
I found it, looked at it, noticed it was looking back.
And the courtship dance began.
It was feathers of stone
smoke and claws
all in a ball of fire, melting the fears into a bubble of
        clear glass.
I found my new gargoyle; he found me back.
I lived before in this town during the Dutch years and
        I was once fed by mother gargoyle
to the hatchling that now dances around me.
Yes, one more time, I want to be devoured by him.
I become the food of the gargoyle.
After he was done, he crawled back around his steeple.
Leaving me behind

satisfied.

III
LOVE AND LUST

A friend of mine invited me to reenact a play that was "Off Broadway" at the time. The play was based on a group of gay friends that decided to get to know each other by playing the game.

I arrived at his apartment on time. Six other guys showed up for the game. The reality is that more than four people is a tight fit, but the idea of six guys playing "Twister" sounded good at the time.

We started by introducing ourselves and saying a little bit about ourselves. Then the game started and every time you lost your balance and fell, you had to answer a very personal question. We really got to know each other very well, pretty soon.

Oh, by the way, did I mention that we were all naked? Those were the days!

FG

ONCE UPON A NIGHT

That night, I thought we were looking at the same
     sky.
We were both so young, and in my mind,
we made love tangled up between stars and heaven's
     dust.
Like the seed of a planet in an artist's hand,
our wish to belong and be loved,
like the peace that covers you after crying,
lying on the grass, the immensity of everything at
     once,
you, like a flame on my skin,
burning, branding the huge need in me…
the same man looking at the same star.

At once, yet many decades ago,
a path chosen,
yet blindly grasped.

TOGETHER THROUGH TIME

From all the loves I have woven in my heart,
your name is written in stars.
From all the tears,
laughter,
growing,
I recognized you from times that went by.
I have been yours,
you have been a part of me
since the birth of the first star.
Because we are the dust that sailed
quietly, with a music
of its own
in the hearts of all orbs,
in the soul of all lust.
With the strength of a million poems
recited at once.
With the touch of all those who have loved
and been loved.
We are the diminutive part of a whole
that speeds through time eternally.
I have been yours before;
you have been mine,
many times.
We are an old song that only we can sing,
a story with many ends,
from many lives
like two mirrors.
You are the comet, I am your trail of lights.

This love is stronger than the power of a seed
or a hymn.
Our love is as old as the silence of any star.

Queen of the Rebel Hearts

I think she was next to me; she held my tired hand.

FG

She walked our ground until last year.
Her name was Rebecca.
You were the queen of our tribe.
We were all intertwined in a web of forgotten verses
within the soul of an old poet's mind.
Your kindness grew attached to each and every one
        of us
and we were all motherly protected by you.
From you, we became the ink that gave birth to our
        collective prose.
Our mother angel who sprouted wings among us,
you traveled through canyons and seas
to select the best of the rebel hearts,
and made us feel safer regardless of your worries
        about mortality.
We all received from you our own right to be wrong
        or right,
even if that meant to slash in sacrifice your own
        hands.
We all were instructed to fight till the end
with the perseverance of this earth's clock.
Rebecca, you brought the day into our hearts.
And scolded the nights away.
We, your handmade rebels, learned to find fire and
        live engulfed in our own light,
nurturing peace of heart.

You made us strong, bold, with the strength of a
     dragon
and the touch of a dove.
You nursed our "todays" and "nows"
and cradled us to sleep under the shadow of the tree
     of life.
Escaping our darkness with the thunders of anger
     from a conquistador.
You nurtured our land and fed our roots,
even if that meant revealing your beautiful scars.
I remember you today, like the soldier mourns the
     dead.
With eyes open and hearts exposed,
you gave birth to the tribe for us.
I miss you, so, Amazon mother earth,
with deep gratitude and loyalty.
From now on,
I will steal the fire from the gods again
and plant its seeds over the land
of the tribe of the rebel hearts.

Burning Urges

Late one night in Riverside Park.
We touch.
No names.
Hunger.
In my apartment,
before I close the door,
we capture the night, ride it till morning.
Both Latinos, from the Caribbean.
His Dominican accent tongue-rolls
a promise of lust.
We jump from Spanish to English,
taking tokes.
Cylinder of glass.
My first time smoking.
My heart beats faster,
my speech slurs.
my pupils dilate,
sunflower follows sun.
My mouth is dry from the reek:
burning plastic,
the smell of coke.

Burning our darkness away,
in the darkness of my room,
interrupted by flashes
from the torch
for this ritual, a night without stars,
spirits from a mythical box.

Night breaks into morning
and morning into day.
All night all day.
This night of riding dragons
we burn human time
in a cylinder of glass.

No regrets.
No need to justify.

Free for All

Burning
I find myself riding.

Waiting
weekends
summer months.
Open the black book, Felix:
names collected in bars,
dark alleys,
bathhouses.

Pick up the phone,
call them:
105th Street and Broadway.
Door closed by 10:00 pm.
Everyone to fuck
till night is fisted by day.

Right on time.
They arrive
one by one.
Thirty seven tonight.
A willing crowd.
Stronger than the hungry god,
herds of satyrs.
Tina, coke, crack, acid,
shrooms, poppers.
Zeus knows what else!
Rum, wine, beer, scotch, gin.

Dante's circle of lust:
the night starts slow.
Then the human wave
floods the bedroom,
the living room, the kitchen, the hall.
Magical touch knows
where to touch.

Games to play:
bottoms
tops
daddy
son
leather man
twink
hairy bear

Ball of fire:
the moon howls horny at the night.
Golden waters baptize,
a shower on dry skin
or thirsty cracked land—
ignites.
Pan blows the flutes;
the centaur pounds the tattooed bear.
I, Bacchus,
in my New York apartment.
Every weekend
the heat of a thousand summers.

FÉLIX GARMENDÍA

My men
kiss
caress
blow
their sounds

A flock of mating gargoyles
on the steeples
of compulsive pining.
All the magic that bursts.

I indulge,
addicted to touch:
men on men.

Guilty

Have I ever interrupted a loving thought?
From fear, from being foreign to that space.
A boy inside a man until later in my life.
To how many "thank-you"s did I never respond?
How many kind acts did I not grasp?
How many times did I block that which joins us?

Out of the selfish place that inflates, then denies the
    self,
I have done so.

How Beauty Refracts

Inside the silence of a broken tear, I remember the
     way it used to be.
The crazy moons, the sleepy suns.

The abundance of pleasure in the spine of every day.
The way it used to be, now a grey feeling.
A muted scream in Van Gogh's ear.
It's similar to the broken promise of eternal beauty,
     that so many of us refuse to let go of.
I, for my life, refuse to see it broken.
I find beauty in the tears of light, in the almighty
     flame, in the sharp edges, in the brilliant
     reflection of a sun every morning.

I refused to believe life was beautiful, in my early
     twenties.
It's a lie that the young carry tangled up in their
     simple lack of years.
There's beauty in every shard of broken smiles,
     forgotten goodbyes and ignored hellos.
The beauty that grows and grows...like the hope of
     the ill and the dance of the deaf.
The beauty that spreads like sparkling sands of
     heavenly bodies.
I believe in beauty with the faith of a fern that
     unravels itself to kiss the light.
The way it is, like the real bird that sings freely, or the
     hidden pearl, unaware of its beauty.

The way it used to be is nothing but a paved road to
    my peaceful today.
The today I love, with the kind of beauty I celebrate.
The today that makes me smile, and gives me strength
    to hold on for another ride.
A ray of light that lends me the lust needed to mount
    my next star.

Hunting Fauns

Through roads and chests I carved my path.
Through the darkness of the dusty gods that fear
     knelt in front of,
to playful cubistic reality: My first encounter with a
     bison.
The cave of lust.
Divine art? Energy and genital scorpion chakra?
Lust.
Lust for satisfying the hungry beast.
Lust for the very same reason we learn to walk,
     crashing on an eager mother's hug.
Lust: The morning light squeezes through the crack
     of dawn.
Lust: nature covered in black gold. The forest of
     hairy chests where I hunted fauns.
Their legs like granite, cracked but triumphant
     covered with weathered man skin that I used
     to caress while kneeling and kissing the stem
     of life.
The perfect silverback line of fur, the holy chest black
     hair crosses, the tree branch veiny arms.
The bearded strength of a deep dark eyed semi god.
The one man show monologue of virility, center
     stage, under the spotlight.
Standing like Lorca in front of the gun.
Discovering all lust,
the lust that slept for two decades, after fearing a god
     fragile as glass.

Lust came as a spray of light and colors through a
        gem, the first time I was touched.
Beauty became lust for men, strength, time.
Life lusted for me as much as I lusted for it.

Lust

Some people are afraid of living,
some develop a hunger for lust.
And talking about lust…
I made it my home.

I'm the red homosexual
I'm the orange teacher
I'm the relentless yellow disabled.
The green Latino- American
The blue liberal
and the purple secular humanist.

I'm a gay rainbow of many convictions.
With all of those tentacles
I etch my trace on wood, like Dürer must have done.
I print my life with words instead,
I want my plates to last.
Desired by many, I desired many more.
I left my fingerprints on many strong backs
in full moons
while answering the primal howling
true to my pack, centered in my truth.

I rolled my dice a few more times than most.
They came up:
branded by skin with LUST.

LUST FOR LOVE

In
early years of manhood,
we became close.

You moved to Europe.
became a professor.
I became a school teacher.
searched for man love.

You consumed your years
in the ephemeral light of your ego,
kneeling against the broken mirror
from fear of love and life.
I became quetzal in love, on my own.

You devalued life
in shining armor over your dead self.
I tried it.
You feared it
all.
You learned books of knowledge.
My skin, drunk with lust,
found pleasures you only read about.
You lived in a bubble,
I thrived dancing around flames;
you became weaker,
I became stronger.
Living,
you forgot about love.

Félix Garmendía   *61*

You searched in dusty pages
what I found on my road.

I grew like a sequoia in dreams,
in strength,
in man to man fiery lust.
And you remained looking for all, in dusty books
till we became old.

I learned from love.
After all those years,
I became sick but remained strong.
You became old and never met love.
You told me,
"your deterioration is overwhelming."
As an answer, I remained strong.
You walked away.
I stayed with love.

Now you call to wake what died,
the forgotten,
the path left behind.
You became weaker.
I grew from pain
but still remained strong.
As you were lost in centuries of books and self-love.

You said you could not see me.
You opened that box.
In front of those words, you fell apart.
I can't forgive you.
You walked away.

You left behind
thirty eight years

then you asked
how I was.

You call from darkness
I answer from light.
This is my answer to your call:
What once grew,
died,
from neglect.
Time to walk away.

Go!

Two Refracted Stars

1984,
my first journey
yet somehow soaked with déjà vu.
Meandering around Venice, recognizing palaces and
     bridges.
They felt familiar, like the instinct used by a mother
     to recognize her child,
or the old song that prompts a smile or a tear.
I was submerged in centuries of art.
Finding myself wearing a feline mask for carnival
or watching a sculpture being born from a block of
     marble.
I walked beside the Grand Canal, gathering refracted
     stars
beneath the Doge's Bridge of Sighs, bathed in the
     lunar light,
I breathed the prisoners' sighs as if they were my own.
I paced familiar ground.
I knew the balconies full of red geraniums,
I flew around Saint Mark's with the resident doves
under a sunset of lace and hand blown glass, with the
     colors of Murano,
and the stoic endurance of a bronze horse.

Nightly, I found myself drawn to a forgotten corner
where an ancient fountain embraced me,
incanting soothing, intimate and familiar hymns.
The waters of Venice,
the life of the city,

the canals,

the veins,

the convoluted vessels of a griffin that refused to die.

The people seemed like ephemeral thoughts hovering
    around a stage much older than they were

with gondolas that came and went,

sailing under bridges I burned long ago to light my
    path.

It was my last night in Venice,

and I returned in a moonless night to say goodbye to
    the forgotten fountain,

firefly stars on the face of the water.

I remembered those rays,

their long, lonely arms reaching through the darkness
    of the moonless night.

One of those arms crashed into my throat, or

maybe it was the vague memory of an old story of
    interrupted love.

Either way, my whole being was immersed in the
    hidden message,

and I cried like a homeless child.

So much I cried that the stars dimmed their light in
    compassion.

And the hidden moon woke up to the murmurs of a
    saddened old fountain

with the message of a centuries old love left behind.

In that moment I looked up at the ancient walls
    framing my departure.

The message was clear.

I wasn't there to say goodbye,
I was there to welcome hopes of finding him among
        refracted tearful stars.
And I promised Venice, at the foot of the fountain,
            that I would return when I recognized him in
            the crowd
one more time.

Thirty four years after, old and fragile now, I live in
            New York.
I found him in another crowd.
Forgive me, Venice. for not fulfilling my promise.
Maybe we will return together
he and I
as refracted stars
to kiss the water of the fountain.

Resolute

It was an immediate attraction,
maybe broken toys can recognize each other.

Both different,
carrying centuries of guilt and pain,
bodies burned by sin clawing at us,
or so we thought:
despair
loneliness
confusion
the Church.
We tried to play love we thought
normal.
But love ran deeper than bodies,
than needs and fears.
Fears of finding out
what was too early touched and branded

Intertwined in despair and regrets.
Submerged in a place
between darkness and the world.
She, fractured everywhere,
a forgotten doll in a dusty attic
starving for light
strength
the healing touch
of a friend.
I, broken too by the man of god.
By the hand of god.

FÉLIX GARMENDÍA   67

Like resolute ivy, we embraced our broken roots,
blossomed in light,
loved over ruins of a demolished wall.

I moved away
but stayed with HER.
Our roots were winged,
played with the clouds across an ocean.
Through the years we grew old but apart.

I called one day and she was gone.
Just like the blink of the blind.
Maybe she returned to the attic.
Maybe she went to where the gods would fix her,
but the real soul print of her remained with me.
I still see her
and very often in our dreams we play.
She seems happier these days.
After laughing together,
we say goodbye again.

When I return to the world
I find my brokenness.
My own shattered self.
And the message is clear.
Please wait for me,
we need to love
we need to rest.
I'm just getting ready
to see you again.

SHADOW

A mere second brings your shadow.
A single fraction of life remembered.
Do you still walk on my fears?
For a second, I feel your heartbeat.
From a distance,
across the precipice filled with old leaves,
you appear in the glitter of my younger time.
A light filled halo, gleaming;
music of that first kiss.
Like you, many left their mark on my skin.
But like few, I grew fond of your explosion:
skin on my skin.
Others faded, a dying echo.
For a second, you walk in my shadow,
dance around my regrets,
young years that brought lust,
life with every stolen smile.
Like yours.
Music of fingers on my back.
Tattoo: the pleasure, little gems threaded through

behind me now.
Shadow.
Those smiles...
evolved a different species: a fern that unfolds to real
        sun, warmest light.

Those years of you
now sit on the ashes of an old fire.

FÉLIX GARMENDÍA   69

Dance to an outdated tune.
For I found love,
the man who guards my steps.

In him, I found myself.

So, old time, older friend,
Fare thee well, shadows halt.

Life is good, thanks for stopping by...
Good bye.

THE FIGHT

How do you fight?
You start to punch ghosts.
You refuse to stop.
You carve your own path
and the white flag flies
over your own interrupted wars,
the demons that touch,
then free you.
Nights of men fill the void
and make you see stars.
You grow up fast.

And then, you taste eternity
the first time your eyes and his
meet in the dark.

The Temple of Sin

I am the original temple of all sin.
Where all forbidden pleasures live and thrive.
Where forgotten "morals," in the name of the
      furious search of happiness, dance around
      the campfires of a cobalt blue *Carpe Diem.*

Today like every day before this one,
I promise to live according to my code of life.
If it's a new land, leave a trail of seeds that will bloom
      the day love will reign supreme again.
If it's beautiful, devour it with eyes.
If it is sensual, caress it until it bleeds the juice of life.
If it's forbidden, make love to it.
If it is dark and wild, tame it with the flame of lust
      and ride it till sundown

when the stars will embrace my lusty gallop
with kisses of light.

IV
HOPE AND FEAR (AIDS)

Yesterday, I came across a very poignant photo. It was a picture taken at a vigil that took place on Christopher Street, N.Y. within the first five years of the AIDS epidemic. Those dark years when we were dying by the thousands and nobody seem to be able to help us, when having HIV was a death sentence, no meds, no knowledge, no hope.

I tested positive for the HIV virus on December 19, 1989 after enduring three years of self-imposed celibacy in order to avoid HIV. Little did I know it was already in me. That was twenty four years ago.

In the early '90s I decided to join one of the AIDS vigils. The ritual was really beautiful and full of conflicting emotions of pain and hope.

We started the vigil at 7th Avenue walking towards the piers. We were all carrying candles in silence. Somehow we managed to place the candles on the river, and we watched them float away until the light died. You could see hundreds of people carrying pictures of loved ones, praying, crying, holding hands with strangers and giving support to those who needed it most.

On our way back to 7th Avenue where we started the vigil, we encountered a sour note.

Right on 7th Avenue a driver in a shiny new blue car screamed at the crowd. "FAGGOTS!" The crowd heard it, but most of us were so involved in the moment that we let it go. One more hater, I said to myself. It was his bad luck that he would find himself stopped by a red light nearby. Right in front of the crowd. In a matter of seconds hundreds of people full of anger and frustration jumped on the blue car, pulled the driver out of his seat and physically turned the car over and totally destroyed it in a matter of minutes, while the crying owner screamed, "I'm sorry, please stop, this is my new car!" I watched the whole thing in astonishment while sitting on a mailbox.

That day I felt very proud of being part of a community that no longer was looking for "tolerance." It was demanding respect.

FG

Bleeding

I used to burn poems,
a very profuse bleeding of words.
I returned them to the universe
to exorcise my pain.

Fear and Hope

In hope we grow
under shadows of fear.
In hope we hurt
during pruning season.

A frenzy of ecstasy:
moaning, carpe diems.
Day by day, a cloud.
Are we alone
or protected by a god's strongest fears?

There used to be a god,
roaming my darkness.
He disappeared.

Now only each other
forcing fate or facing destiny
wherever we belong.

Invited to the harvest festival,
I savor the lagoon of seven sins.
With hopes of living
just a bit longer.

In spite of illness,
I become the host
of the feast.
Hope
in the face of fear.

On My Own

I detached myself from you, after feeling your
      absence.
After noticing that life continued,
when most wouldn't dare to attempt to live apart
      from you.
Life on my own became the rule.
You weren't there when I was born with the original
      sin. I didn't hold a chance from day one.
Early in my life,
you were absent when your followers fractured my
      will to live.
You were not around when your people threw
      garbage at my house screaming "faggot" for
      speaking my mind
and
when my uncle, in your name, described me, while
      drunk, as a criminal at the early age of 10.
Or when my grandfather pushed me away when I
      went to kiss him good night.
Where were you?
Your nothingness is a scar in my mind.
Your absence burned my hopes.
You cast shadows over my fragile pride, and made me
      feel guilty for being alive.
Was it you or your followers?
Either way, you both watched and did nothing.
You looked the other way when one of your
      messengers on earth startled my 15-year-old
      skin.

One more time, when life showed me its fangs, you
        didn't stop your people's fists.
You didn't comfort me after I was branded with the
        ritual that marks us all with your "damaged
        goods" seal.
I was supposed to feel protected,
but when I searched for love, AIDS found me.
I became a ticking bomb.
A bomb of anger and guilt for believing the lie,
I felt defeated and forgotten one more time.
Receiving a death sentence in 1989, I decided to
        burn my candle from both ends.
And life without you gave me the biggest pleasures
        of this earth.
During the pandemic,
I wasn't the only flame fighting the wind;
most embraced the night too early while begging you
        for one more day to live.
Am I supposed to thank you for making me a survivor
        when most of my friends departed early?
Were you around in their last moments?
I bet you were busy.
For how long are you going to let people castigate us
        with your name in their mouths?
Your absence has been long and I have no interest in
        mentioning your name.
I reject the notion that you ever existed, otherwise
        you would be the unanswered question.
Thorns in my eyes.
I have been without you for decades now.
I thought about feeling sorry for your followers,
but I was too busy healing from their actions in your

absence.
This is me, stone carved by the wind.
In my own name I became my self-contained miracle,
dirt, water and seed.

Recalled to Life (Dr. Russell)

Your name still gives me strength, Dr. Russell.
Those short days, long nights.
1980s to 1995.
Years of death.

You set me on the new time machine that added
        years to my life.
Protease inhibitors.
We met at gay bars,
discussed blood tests, T cells
between sips of frozen margaritas
while smiling and looking at the boys.
For every new issue, you had an answer.
"Life is all about today," you said,
"and what we want it to become."
Pure solace in the eye of the storm.

Years went by and I blossomed, resurrected,
into a strong body and mind.
Magical doctor,
I sent my friends to you.
Some managed to thrive; others passed.
You were a welcome, bright, glorious moon
looming over long bleak terrain.
But in our last visits you seemed spent,
weary except for your strong warm bear hug.

One day you left, shut down emotionally.
Although you did not answer me,

you left me safe at the living side of the bridge.
Then, on Fire Island, you showed up.
"Felix, I burned out."
I read it in your eyes.
You tried to save us all.

Your spirit was crushed by losing so many lives.
Like watching people drown
or slowly bleed to death, unable to intercede.
Alone in your Brooklyn apartment,
you took the final step.
Your "doctor pad" bore the prescription
that ended your anguish.
When I learned of your departure
I struggled, trying to understand.
You became the sacrificial pyre
where old red oaks kissed the air with ashes,
lighting the night of the ones you tried to save
by kissing their ashes to the sky.
Like the weak elephant, the once tireless and mighty,
you headed home to die.
It hurt like knives
until I remembered:
"Life is what you make of it."

Goodbye, but not goodbye,
angel of so many.
You are always with me.

FÉLIX GARMENDÍA

Sentenced to Life

December 19, 1989.
We are decorating the tree.
"Mr. Garmendía, your test for HIV came back
        positive."
Time stops.
For a second I remain on the phone.
Fear screams through our eyes.
Rick gives me a hug.
The 7th floor balcony
offers a solution.
Instead, I fall asleep.

The second test confirms it.
I, an art teacher, sculptor of lessons,
create tears during one lesson.
My contract is not renewed.
The second doctor's cold voice: A year and a half at
        most.
The cold New York rain and my tears
wet the pavement,
drench my shattered peace further.
The sadness rends my bones.
My friends start to disappear.
One by one.
No details, they're just gone.
The great old sequoias fall apart in eternal night.
I make friendships that last a few months.
Surreal *Carpe Diems.*
Beautiful souls leave without saying goodbye,

like the melody from an old broken guitar
that disappears after a turn.
Thank you, Ronald Reagan:
For ignoring us.
For the hate.
For the civil war between our will to live and
        agonizing death.
For those of us
abandoned like old dogs.

This is how it was, the terrible years:
First, the AZT almost killed us.
We said what we thought were last prayers.
But then protease inhibitors revived us
and hope.
As for me,
Dr. Russell, more than a doctor,
showed me how to survive
and made the shadows disappear
as we laughed at them.
Until one day he disappeared too.

My husband and the few friends AIDS spared
fed my will to live against all odds.
And I now conclude:
I was meant to leap from victim to storyteller.

It's 2018 now, 30-plus years.
I still remember: The ones that left too early,

FÉLIX GARMENDÍA   83

the sobbing families,
the ones who died homeless.
I survive, covered in names and scars,
not wondering anymore.

Love and luck collide.
I ask, stop asking, ask again.

Knowing the final answer, I ride life bareback
and tame the beast.

Songbird

While the hurt songbird sleeps,
the morning breaks.
Seeds sprout, things grow.
Invisible silence of new clouds
cushions the order
of the forest.

It will be all right.

V
GAY OUT
LOUD

"By night, love, tie your heart to mine, and the two together in their sleep will defeat the darkness."

PABLO NERUDA

Coming Out Day

For those who fear the light, for those who live in
    the dark.
A thousand different reasons, with shadow of excuses.
Fear is the culprit.
Fear of hurting others, even though we ourselves live
    our lie.
Fear of church and gods, even though we are living
    in the dark.
Fear of not being accepted, by whom, by what?

I came out in the '80s.
We belong to a group of brave people, warriors.
I will never go unnoticed, under the radar
like melting snow from car exhaust.
Braveness, like an Olmec head or an Easter Island
    moai.
The sun of pride and the moon of self-respect.
We light our way through the darkness
with the luminous ashes of those burned to death—
    fagots.
Faggots.
So many fought alone.
Against the "norm."
History has taught us.
Those who stood in the spotlight brought marriage
    equality.
Edie Windsor, the halo on our rainbow,
the celebration of life, to stand with your "one,"
to hold their hand. PRIDE!

Félix Garmendía   *89*

In front of the world.
We become one,
face the light.
We disperse the shadows,
ignorance about us.
LGBTQ, come out!
Wake up and punch the light.
October 11 shines all around.

Gay Poem

Persecuted, harassed and crucified.
From eternities that have gone by.
I was born to love my kind.
I was born to embrace and sleep on strong chests.
My hands,
my eyes,
my aura shines bright when I kiss a man.
From the earliest memories to my present,
I have always touched them like it was going to be
my last time.
With the eagerness that only my kind can ignite.
I like their arms like trees that reach my skies.
I love their eyes, their minds, their smiles.
They heal my age and make me young against my
time.
I was born to love a man. I was born to love my kind.

The Colors of Wrath

At 1:20 a.m. on Saturday June 28, 1969, at the
       Stonewall Inn in Greenwich Village, New
       York,
the anger of thousands of years erupted.
It was the moment when liberty screamed and my
       people exploded against the homophobic
       cops with rage.
Six days of anger in defense of our right to be happy,
to be part of the American dream, "With Liberty and
       Justice for all."
A group of drag queens and queers defended their
       right to be.
Tired of the establishment abuse, they used their
       high heels, rocks, and fists
as weapons against the blue wall of intolerance and
       hate.
My people were tired of being mocked and
       disrespected, some said depressed by the
       recent death of Judy Garland.
It was a quiet morning at the Stonewall Inn when
       the world's anger was defeated by the bravery
       of the LGBT.
Those six days of contentious spirits in a civil war out
       of a recently opened Pandora's box.
After six days the cops were defeated; they were
       forced to back up by my brave warriors.
We won the battle, now let's go and win the war.
It's the day we channel the Spartan in us. And we
       sprinkle the streets with rainbows.

And about the opened Pandora's box?
We will forever grow with the strength of hope.

II

May 12th to Sunday June 30th, 2019,
gold for the 50th anniversary.
"WORLD PRIDE" in New York, Stonewall's home,
as the memory of the gay rights warriors
overflows the streets with our rainbow hearts:
Red
Orange
Yellow
Green
Blue
and Purple for our conviction
we will achieve equal rights.
The fight continues.

VI
NEW YORK
HOME

Washington Heights is home, where respect for differences becomes the norm.

Thank you, New York, for adopting me! Thank you for infusing me with life and teaching me how to sing my song in rainbow colors.

FG

Mabon

The summer is dead.
I can hear the earth feeding on the green leaves.
It's that time of the year again, where falling leaves
        are cradled down by the crisp winds,
to wrap safely the seeds of spring with the quilt of
        fall.
Resting on the pavement, covering the land with
        orange, red, yellow and brown patches of
        organic cloth.
The earth's palate responds to the sun's farewell.
And the fairies dance and harvest to the tune of
        Mabon.
The sun's distance paints the trees with fire.
In the eyes of humans,
all butterflies become moths.
Playing children, frolicking fawns.
A walk in the park makes me recite the monologue
        of autumn.
Deep inside, many questions reincarnate:
Can we consider fall a form of death?
Do we understand either one?
Do we ever return like spring does after winter?
During early fall we sense the glorious demise of the
        summer's heat welcoming the colors of the
        sacred flaming gnomes.
Is this stroll through Central Park following the route
        of my life?
I don't think I know the answer to that question yet.
And that is OK.

FÉLIX GARMENDÍA

My New York state of mind: Central Park on the
first night of fall.

My Favorite/*Mi Favorita*

Lin-Manuel Miranda, Ron Perlman, Dr. Ruth…
I moved to Washington Heights in 2002,
a little art deco, green patch of ancient trees,
the northern tip of Manhattan's iron glove.
The last holocaust survivors, their numbered wrists
       branded by hate.
The nuns from Mother Cabrini's shrine.
The Bolivian lady collecting cans.
The Dominican kids skateboarding the street.
"Bela" with her wheelchair-bound husband.
In a restaurant.
My husband Denis left for a moment.
Bela asked me, "Do you speak Spanish?"
I answered in Spanish, *"Sí."* Her face lit up.
A face chiseled by lines of a hard life.
Wearing a babushka,
grey skirt, black sweater.
Black shoes, a simple diamond wedding ring.
She ordered food for her unresponsive husband.

"I am 'Bela' with one 'l,' but here in New York,
'Bella.'
My Orthodox Polish Jewish parents escaped
to Mexico City
in the '30s."
Her Spanish lilted the sound of an old Mexican
       ballad.
As she fed her husband
she asked about my wheelchair.

Félix Garmendía   *99*

In Mexico City, she said,
a rat bite put her in one.
She told me, "I understand."
And it echoed through me:
A disabled, gay, Puerto Rican, atheist man,
an Orthodox, elderly Jewish woman, born in Mexico,
now feeding her disabled German husband.
Where else but in Washington Heights?

When Denis returned,
we both watched her push her husband
with the ancient strength of a bronze sculpture.

From now on, we would say hello.

The Date (9/11)

It is the name we all remember.

The spine of humanity was broken,
as living missiles killed the fragile peace of the planet.
We all froze in horror
at the stench of death
coming from the guts of despair;
we watched it happen a thousand times.
TV was a broken record, repeating two numbers
        with a dash.
Nothing but sirens flying downtown.
People crying in the streets,
some covered in dust, all submerged in a pool of
        sadness.
People wandering around, looking to the sky.
Some running, others praying, all of us shattered.

The day America was forced to kneel.

VII
A NEW
CHALLENGE
(INCLUSION
BODY
MYOSITIS)

"The roar of pain is either art or revolution."

QASIM CHAUHAN

CARPE DIEM VINES

I know the pain of the runt, the born weak, when the
    vultures start to close on us and the rest just
    watch.
For those reasons and more, my childhood danced
    on the blade of a fast goodbye.
Puberty arrived and the side show began.
I became the freak, laughing stock.
And from ashes of wanting to live, I rose like white
    smoke.
I became:
a singer and a bard.
A teacher,
an actor.
I walked away from goodbyes.
Then, in my early twenties,
HIV menaced.
The scent of goodbye returned.
With the rage of a surviving lover, left alone after a
    long fight,
I refused the scent,
refused to drown in a swamp of goodbyes.
Even with everyone around me departing,
leaving empty chairs in the support group,
like a dying plant in a closed apartment
when the last ray of light vanishes.

Instead I became the thriving virus's pulse under
    hibernation, living when it touched life.
The ancient seed refused to die.

FÉLIX GARMENDÍA   *105*

Then fate struck again.

Something called Inclusion Body Myositis,
the newest threat.
Auto immune condition, inflammation of the
        muscles until destruction:
weakness,
early disability.
No treatment.
No cure.
Wheelchair.
And the stench of goodbye came back.
One more time I fought.

I began to love someone who loved me,
Our ardor a fuel to stop time.

I am 57 now, with HIV,
with inclusion body myositis:
wheelchair bound,
left arm paralyzed, typing with one finger
on my right hand.
I look at myself in the mirror without escape,
slowly consumed in body, yet growing wings in
        strength.
Different time, different struggle.
Same grownup, once scared child.
I have learned to live tangled up in *Carpe Diem* vines.
But the signs and scent of leaving must wait.
I'm not ready to go just yet.

NEST

Sometimes it frustrates me,
depending on him for EVERYTHING.
I was independent, had an active life.
A job, many friends.
All gone but him.
That's the nature of migrant birds.

The past turned to dust, time invested in him.
Against all odds,
we survived the bad weather.
I, safe in the nest he built.

Nomad

We walk this earth, nomads of time
with breathing wounds that mark our lives.
We live and lock horns with some; with most, we
       smile or even make love.
Against the power of all words that make things true,
I proclaim my own truth; Against all bumps on the
       road
I walk with breathing wounds.

Passion for Life

passion love
life
unpredictable,
borrowing fire and forging hopes
through ups and downs.
My unpredictability embraces life;
life embraces the unpredictable.

Still in the Fight
(Inclusion Body Myositis)

In the '80s,
the AIDS conflagration
charred friend and foe alike.
A few of us survived.

One more time
fighting for my life
my soul-bird
flies out the window scared.
My soul escapes;
my body
alive upon the pyre.
This body, once sculpted
within an inch of its life,
admired, desired,
now robbed even of back muscles.

A new threat.
One more time,
my body is attacked,
with the jealousy of a god's wrath.
Like Hephaestus, the son of Zeus thrown out of
        Olympus,
tumbling down the hill
and crashing on my pride.
The smell of death returns.

Fighting for life
against deteriorated windmills—my arms.
Legs that stooped my walks around fairy land.
Sitting forever.

I will never walk again.
Half of my body, dead,
rots away like road kill
under the summer sun;

my left is clipped, broken,
the right arm gives up the fight.

I keep on—
dragging my wheels,
wearing shoes that never touch the ground.

Now my feet fly forever.

17 years.
The bird takes flight
in the keyboards of my mind.
Silent scream
strong
for those I love.
I will not leave this earth
silently defeated.

FÉLIX GARMENDÍA   *111*

I sing the lyrics of my anthem
to praise hope
instead of a petty angry god.

STILL ALIVE

This journey began in 2001.
My body used to be sculpted.
Trained by the best.
Admired.
Until that moment when the weight of life
crushed me with its boulder
and my soul-bird
flew out of the window scared.
My soul escaped
my body
when placed alive upon the pyre.
Inclusion Body Myositis was the new bandit
that stole from my body even the muscles of my back.
A new threat.
One more time,
my body was attacked,
with the jealousy of a god's wrath.
And the downhill road began.
Like Hephaestus, the son of Zeus thrown out of
        Olympus,
tumbling down the hill
and crashing on my pride.
The smell of death returned.
And it took me back to the '80s
during the HIV conflagration
that burned and charred
friends and hope alike.
Until a few of us
survived god's wrath.

FÉLIX GARMENDÍA   113

One more time
fighting for my life
against the deteriorated windmills of my arms.
And the legs that stooped my walks around my fairy
         land.
There I was,
sitting forever,
to never be able to walk again.
Half of my body was dead.
Attached to the living parts.
Rotting away like road kill
Under the summer sun,
fighting for my life.
One more fucking time.
About my wings or so-called arms:
Left one is clipped and broken forever,
the right arm very much giving up the fight.
And I keep going on,
dragging my wheels
wearing shoes that will never touch the ground.
It's been 17 years down this path.
One more time I start to tell my story,
a story with no end nearby.
A long story so far that stung me on the core of my
         pride.
I learned many lessons on the way.
I learned to replace the broken song with a bird in
         flight.
I learned to write on the keyboards of my mind.
I wrote and revived poems from years gone by.
I learned to scream in tears,

biting my silence.
I must be strong
for husband, family and friends alike.
Because I will not leave this earth silently defeated.
I will remain strong.
Believing in science.
Not a hungry deity.

The Broken Doll

I know of an old doll that sits in its chair.
It quietly looks at nothing with green glass eyes.

Beautifully dressed, beautifully kept.
It stares at me, every day
eye to eye, from within.
If I take it out to play, I do so carefully, taking care of
      its broken porcelain limbs.
Keeping the pieces together with hope and glue.
The doll asked me today if it could go alone to play.
I told him, no.
Eye to eye.
We are bonded forever.
You will never go out
to play by yourself,
anymore.

THE DREADED TIME

There's anger erupting from my pores.
The kind of anger that has been tied and gagged for
      many years now.
The frustration that grows, a fungus in the dark,
and sprouts, a thorny vine that cuts my throat.
My body comes too close to the nothingness
that every disabled body fears and hates.
After years of fighting, I find myself sad, looking
      inward.
The outside, ravaged by ugliness only I can see.
Linens and silks that hide the thin and broken limbs,
the unborn blisters of the dying smile.
The loud screams of silence that deafen the voices of
      all deities.
Bowing my head,
I hear
the god of decaying bodies knocking at my door,
the stillness of a heart that skips a beat.
That scream at the sight of my image on the mirror
      of my eyes.
Not fighting the aging process, I rather watch the
      broken clock that like me, has already stopped.

Time will tell. It's always about time.
And I will keep on hiding behind prisms of hungry
      hopes, withered smiles and deaf songs.

FÉLIX GARMENDÍA   *117*

The Embrace

I want to embrace the broken toy
that is in a dark corner hurting.
I want to meet those who think differently
crowned by the virtue of respect.
I want to visit your reality
and try to dance to your favorite tune.
Because everything is possible
when we believe we are all connected.
Somehow the same.
Like roses in one plant
or feathers of a wing.
Like clouds that frolic around the same sky.
We are more similar than different;
we all live, love, lie, forgive or not and die,
and in between we chase dreams
and sprout wings to reach the stars.
To all of those who want to heal with me,
visit my darkness.
I will be there waiting for you
and pointing at that place
where my light shines brightly.

THE RED CANDLE

Inside a green starburst ceramic lantern,
there's a flickering flame that has been burning for
        days and nights.
It used to stand tall and full of life, inside its glass
        tower filled with molten red wax.
Inside its glass body, just like mine, there is red wax.
Like my more fragile glass tower filled with blood,
the candle has been burning for so long it's starting to
        look like a little miracle.
Within us all there's a burning candle that reminds us
        to live life brightly.
What we decide to burn will not block our path;
even pain can give us light.
Some get to listen to the flame within;
others leave it behind and cuddle with darkness.
Regardless of our will to live or die,
the flame will burn until its last dance.
We might as well share our light:
Those who swallow life fully get to reflect shooting
        stars.
Since life is about burning our candle, and like this
        one in my lantern, I refuse to die.
As long as there is red wax remaining in my votive
        candle,
you will find a beating heart.
Our daily struggles strive to conquer them, projecting
        light even against every broken mirror
and make it look like a fistful of stars.

The Void

I know it might seem strange.
Like the first time the word "death" was explained
  to us.
Similar to the confusion of Babel without the
  mystique of a myth.
It seems a bit strange to me, too.
The paths we crossed to fill that void.
The void that feeds on ghosts and unspoken answers.
The void whose hunger can devour a million silences
  and dissolve a tear hidden in the rain.
We fill the void with withered hopes.
We sacrifice doves on the altars of fear and uncertain
  states of mind.
"The Void" that screams like herds of souls in search
  of justice.
The "justice" that flies away before the arrow touches
  it.
We all fill the void, some with thorns, and some with
  petals.
Others with dried up dirt that finds the light behind
  the dark.
In search of food we plant the seed, in search of hope
  we free our birds.
Then we play hide and seek with ourselves.
We all keep on trying to fill the void that only time
  will fill in truth.
It's only human to seek for stars up there where the
  dark reigns as night.

VIII
FLYING ON INVISIBLE WINGS

The almost prismatic beauty of a Monet is magical. I live in NYC, where we have "The Museum Mile" hosting some of the most celebrated pieces of art in the world. One of my favorites is "Reflections of Clouds on the Water-Lily Pond" by Monet. This magnificent piece consists of three panels. The entire piece measures over 40 feet long by almost 7 feet tall. It's enormous! It's part of the permanent collection of the MOMA (Museum of Modern Art). It's also presented alone in a gallery where your eyes, in a fantastic trickery of art, lose themselves into splashes of light, color and reflections.

The first time I saw it, I was confronted with beauty and artistic magnificence. The feeling was overwhelming. The water was so "real" to the point that it seemed to be moving.

Now, going back in the story. Earlier

that day, on my way to the museum, I made a stop in Central Park. It was a beautiful summer day, beautiful sky, beautiful surroundings, and in harmony with nature just in the middle of a huge city like NYC. The world was perfect.

I crossed the park, made a stop behind some old tree, and crossed Fifth Avenue on my way to my lilies. I sat alone on one of the sitting facilities offered by the museum for the full enjoyment of this masterpiece.

I sat and swam amongst lilies, felt the fresh air on my face, engulfed the vibrant colors that the light made glisten like jewels, and had a mystical experience with this impressionist painting. I was very thankful for my short stop in Central Park, where I indulged in one of my favorite pastimes. I'm sure many of you are wondering "what was that?" For those of you who know me, it's not that much of a mystery. The time was 4:20 p.m.

FG

Spring flowers in Fort Tryon Park take on the colors of
the Northern Lights. As you go up the hill to the Cloisters
in summer, unicorns meet you and millions of people
from all over the world. During fall, deeper magic colors
the leaves before winter skies turn cold and low in blue
and white and grey. Denis and I greet them all, I from
my chair, he from behind me as he wheels me into the
park. It is our outside home now.

FG

A PARK FOR ALL SEASONS (WHEELCHAIR MAGIC)

In 2012, the background for our wedding pictures.
Fort Tryon Park, a musical note:
colors borrowed from a fauve painting by Matisse.
The George Washington Bridge at sundown.
The two of us wedding-fine
with good friends,
laughing.

Then, Denis, my husband, and I,
all year long.
Park spirits,
alone together.

Some days so quiet you could hear
the clouds.

II

Winter sweeps back as I fall.
I will not walk again.
My body chooses
to fly
in my chair.

Icicles magic the bareness.
Life continues:
100-year-old maple trees
harvest peace.

Spring comes late.
At the annual Medieval Festival
I am a unicorn (on wheels).
I play with other people's dogs.
In winter
I admire the feral cats' resilience.

It's 2018; six winters have passed,
and now it is autumn.
Some birds leave;
the trees power up
for their show.

And I reign from my wheelchair throne.
The park is my domain
in all seasons.
Like the park, Denis and I,
we grow old together,
ancient trees that relentlessly endure.

Like the feral cats,
I am the owner of my path.

Self Portrait in
Red and Black

Hanging next to a window,
gilt framed,
a painting
from the '60s.
On the canvas,
a man
in his fifties,
round face,
pale skin,
green eyed,
white silky ermine white goatee,
brown Stetson fedora hat,
emerald eyebrow piercing,
gold ruby ring.
dressed in black and red.
He likes fine clothing:
linen, fine jewelry and paisley silks.
This painting, overall bright
like a Goya,
but with somber, dark overtones.
The noble personage
sporting a bowtie,
a diamond art deco stick pin,
black silk sports jacket,
resplendent red floral print shirt.
A burgundy pocket square.
Mondrian pattern socks,

pristine black lizard skin oxford shoes
that have never touched the ground.
He sits in his chair,
a gentleman from another time
living within the frame.
I know him well.
I drive the wheels of his chair.

For the man in the wheelchair, in red and black,
is my self portrait.

Starry Night

Today I touched the sky.
I danced with Van Gogh's swirls on a starry night.
Like thunder, life became intense in the last days.
Unexpected.
Unpredictable.
I found myself swimming in dark waters,
and fear grew like an aroused zenith.
I was under water, submerged,
like 56 years ago in a calla lily womb.
This time I was drowning in the "unfairness" of life.
Listen to me. Do I have the right to point fingers at
        life?
I:
The same artist who played with love and
somewhere in space, found the one.

I became the one that only added to one, remains
        one.
My apologies, life.
It was unfair for me to plant sad seeds on your
        lands.
I open my hand and present it to the night sky.
It's my way of painting swirls in my dark nights.
And the night grew roses in my hands.
But:
How long the life span of a rose?
Here I go again, measuring human time
when my skin is blooming with flowers and wings
in a forever dance with fate and a starry night sky.

The Door to Wonderland
(Happy Smoking Time 4:20)

My present worries,
away they go.
Sprouting dandelions,
little yellow fireworks
under my bare feet,
world
of gnomes, singing sphinxes and fawns,
music.
Time slows down,
the earth smiles.
I can walk again,
leaving wheelchairs behind.
I juggle stars.
I sing.
I cover myself with misty air,
I hang crystal prisms in the branches from trees of
        glass,
playing.
I keep on dancing:
centaurs, birds, purple lady bugs, everywhere.

I stop missing those who left.
I stop being ill.
I escape.
To a green moss-covered field
where my mind talks to the moon.
I play during the day

with the snail's trail of stars.
At night I talk to playful unicorns.
Are those spirits of the dead?
Lights of magic or simply fireflies?
In my sky, I ride kaleidoscopic rays of light
and pink clouds.
I play hide and seek with brightly colored quasars.
Neverland.
I enjoy.

My Red Rose Frida
(Incarnation)

Frida flows in my veins.
She inhabits my soul.
Like beautiful original sin,
her passions are my passions.
I live in her, surrounded by her.
Her art celebrates my life.
With her arms,
my withered arms embrace again.
Her strength becomes my strength.
Our legs don't matter; we have wings to fly.
Her heart keeps me alive, blood red blossom:
tree of life.

IX
PEACE
AND
OTHER
THOUGHTS

Vincent Van Gogh showed me that even a mind in turmoil is capable of giving birth to a star.

FG

ANGELS

I honor those who departed by keeping a light alive
    in our memory.
With the enormous hope of a marching vigil, I keep
    them alive somewhere.
Candle by candle,
tear to dirt,
smoke to infinity.
Remembering the significant happenings, laughing
    or crying at the feet of sunny moments or
    shadows.
I remember because forgetting is not an option.
I grew attached to those I still remember
ivy to wall,
blood to pavement,
stain to saddened soul.
They are with me day and night,
present all the time like the stars behind the sun and
    the sun behind the howling full moon.
There is no day or night for those who departed.
Their presence is in absence like the thin air of
    mountain tops.
How much I wish to understand that real matter
    never dies;
it's only the abandoned house that decays and
    becomes engulfed by the wild weeds of absence,
    that makes me hurt.
Meanwhile, the old spruce keeps on growing and the
    city flows untouched.
Because life continues, even when human time stops

FÉLIX GARMENDÍA

for some.

I have touched many without knowing it was our last
        drink, dance, joint together.

The last trip to Fire Island.

The last embrace naked.

Against all gods and humans, I pledge to never forget
        them.

My crosswords of names and smiles, punches of light
        against the mirrors of life.

That still in absence light each day by day.

The Bullfight

The skin of our country is raw from anger,
the kind of anger that hurts the peace of all living
      things,
the kind of sorrow that shoots blood like the last
      stabbing of an innocent beast by a matador.
Uncertainty rules the red land.
A toreador is circling, like a hungry shark, our pivotal
      human rights.
Fear
Angst
Sorrow
Wrath.
The ones that fight are dying from exhaustion and
      returning like a blue flame.
A flame that touches and consoles the foundation of
     a hurting and agonizing land.
The ones that remain quiet are facing the darkness
      and living half-lives,
hibernating during war.
My body is old, my voice trembles, my arms can't
      reach the arms of my loved ones.
I feel helpless.
We are divided, like never before.
It is like walking in the darkness while shooting at a
      broken moon without aim or light.
Our country is hurting like the bull that fought the
      final sword in the bullfight. Half dead like the
      abandoned soldier,
victim of everything that is wrong but looks right.

Félix Garmendía

The killing of our land has begun.
When does the bullfight stop?

ABOUT THE UNSPOKEN

What to do with the unsaid words?
The ones you mute out of pride or fear,
anger
resentment
confusion.
How to undo the mistake?
Death. The final page in the book.
The one that marks forever unspoken.
How about the poem born when injustice occurs?
Then the silence that slashes like a blade our calm,
        and cuts the vocal cord when anger strikes?
Speak the now:
Poem.
Gesture.
Song.
To heal and give healing back.

Forgive the rest; a bird can't fly backwards.
One more time:
Felix, are you listening?

CUFF LINK BLUES

Boredom and compulsive shopping are like Romulus and Remus: the angry wolf of instant gratification. The mother of a "quick high." I just FUCKING love it!

FG

Parallel stripes of blue and black, framed by silver
        bands.
Two of them, face to face duplicated cells of lapis and
        onyx.
The Mexican craftsman who created you must have
        felt very proud;
it reads "Taxco."
Square shape, shining light reflected on clean silver,
belonging to another time. The century of male
        glamour.
The two like Picasso's young girl looking in a mirror;
duplicate whisper of a lover, twice-spoken desire.
Aristocratic seriousness bordering on sad.
Formidable in shape and craft, from another time.
I remember the ones dad owned. Simple, elegant
        with yellow amber caps.
These, in symmetry of blue and black, with the
        elegance and seriousness of a maritime flag.
An accent of the urgency to decorate, anoint myself
with the armor of fashion.
Dark depressed blue of a Van Gogh night sky.
The serious line of black, framing the cobalt gold
        speckled lapis moments.

I will wear them today, recalling dad in his elegant
    time.

I am there now, one with the harmony of
blues and
everyday life,
bands of onyx, lapis and gold;
the sheen of night clouds
like my cuff links.

Fear

I fear no man, no curse of god.
After years of slavery I found and owned my soul.
No dark words touch my heart.
Only love makes me smile.
Decades on this earth have taught me to survive the
    winters of my mind,
the autumns of my age, and the future of my nights.
I fear no darkness, dogmas or chains.
In the sunset of every day, I rest my head safely to
    sleep
between the arms of my loving man.
I do not judge or accuse others of living their lives.
I have learned to live without a god, his sins,
followers' words that slash like knives.
I fear no evil, I fear no hell or heaven promised for
    "chosen" ones.
I fear no one who thinks differently,
or prays or lies.
My life is full of yesterdays that showed me through
    days and nights,
my present alive in my hands.
I have learned to be without regrets.
I have enjoyed living
without the fear of hell, the absence of light.
Standing on my tired feet, I look ahead
past the fire of guilt, resentment and hate.
Here I am, another day, another chance,
no one to forgive myself
as I can.

I fear no death, I fear nothing but lack of will
to keep up with the fight.

Frozen Steps

My inert feet are like an ancient dragonfly in amber.
They remain quiet upon the untraveled roads.
Like tired old men, they remember the scent of
       unanswered smiles,
the hunger for those roads never touched by my cold
       skin.
And the brightly colored steps that brought me, 21
       LIFE years ago, to him.
My feet are solid bedrock, like those of the Sphinx.
Like those that are awakened outside and inside yet
       chained to a dream.
My steps are whispers that dance in the night,
       without music,
without light.
Against all fears of stumbling in the dark.
My feet, on their way to remember the unanswered
       questions of those roads left behind.

Enough!

In search of peace.
The elusive bird, almost extinct.
The shattered mirror that cries with fractured light.
We keep on searching.
Every day.
With thirst for justice and angst
for another fight against time.
Our rainbows are decomposing
into bitter tears of angry fear.
Our trees are falling, our skies are blurry,
and our colors are fading.
Too many of our children are being slaughtered,
and we fight over ideas.
While young blood sticks to the pavement
of shame and gets devoured by hungry flies.
Meanwhile, we keep on marching.
We keep on screaming
and raising our fists
and screaming our truths,
until no one has to hide
from the bullets of misguided "rights."

My Truth

I find peace in letting go of names that hurt.
Letting go of hurt that names
guilt or regrets.
All the sparks of lonely nights, touching men I
    barely met.
A dance more than a hunt, between a hungry
    hunter and a willing fox.
When our politics or religious views clashed
friends broke up, words were yelled,
families never spoke again.

I hereby let go of all. I have already learned the
    lesson,
and I harvest the fruit.
Let the vultures devour the carcass and clear the
    way.
I leave behind the compulsive search, group
    epiphanies, conversions.
My personal truth might be transitory,
like the blade of the cold breeze of winter, next to
    the soft edge of a spring's rose.
Weeks apart, the same face.

But let my nomad mind wander, unfettered,
through old age,
the maze of life.

MY SEVEN GLORIOUS SINS

For a second, I found myself walking
down to sadness and regrets.
I remembered a few promises
that I will never fill.
I find myself barefoot,
guilty of living and trying.
Cursing on my way to broken glass.
I apologize to Venice for not returning
with the love of my life
like I promised one night
while captive of the Grand Canal
and the curious stars.
I apologize to that student
whose question I couldn't answer.
I apologize for the anger
that clouded my message to a friend.
I apologize to the butterfly I pinned
to an insect collection.
I present to you
my lust for living.
My greed for accumulating
and keeping old souls around me.
My sloth in not repeating myself
to the simple minded.
My wrath against bigotry.
My envy of comets that leave a trail
of lights.
My pride of loving other men.

And
my hedonistic gluttony
for pleasures: mind and flesh.
Finding myself trying to mend "wrongdoing."
Happens every morning before the light
and every evening before the dark.

A list of broken dreams.

If

If this were my last poem, I would want to let all
　　birds sing before finishing it.
If these were my last words, I would like to write
　　them with the dust of comet tails and pin them
　　forever between clouds flying crystals of melted
　　quartz rain.
If life quietly slipped away, I would want to assure
　　myself my message has been spread, in the
　　same way the mist that grows in the morning
　　simultaneously over the wild daisy and the
　　dragonfly wings.
I would wish to plant seedlings.
I would wish to sing my last verses riding a Tiffany
　　orange glass cloud over a Venice sundown by
　　the Grand Canal.
If these were my last written thoughts, I would like
　　to concur with life about the intrinsic goodness
　　of all human beings.
I would want to talk about the craving for melting
　　myself with a mirror image that invited me in.

I met along the crossroads of life:
The interrupted story that once created the big bang
　　that created the five of us, those I call my
　　family.
Those who claimed me as friend.
Science, for extending my life after a death sentence
　　from AIDS.

Those long nights gasping for air intoxicated in drugs
and lust,
the highest of flesh-won pleasure on my search for
solace
in the eye of the HIV storm.
Lands and men I placed my flag on, the flag of trust
that sprouted ferns and bromeliads in the
rainforest habituated by bird quasars
and firefly meteor showers of deep peace and comfort.
The power of a teacher, the Diogenes of knowledge,
the farmers of intellectual growth.
The universe, my last unanswered question,
the last frontier where faith, truth and uncertainty
coexist, like the thirsty lion that drinks water
peacefully next to the trusting zebra.
Art guiding my steps through the foggy mazes of life.
Those who fought before me in the spirit of the 1969
Stonewall.
The pining for men, which gave me roots deeper and
stronger than the place where the diamond
melds.
The voice that evolution gave me 57 years ago.
Denis, the husband who grabbed love and flamed my
life with it, 21 years ago; my legs when mine
could no longer touch the ground.
My inner tunnels, gardens, my windows, balconies
and crypts.
Ambitious, unpredictable, never easy life.

X
THE NAMES
PROJECT
AIDS
MEMORIAL
QUILT

More than 50 tons of tear-stitched community folk-
    art.
The idea was born from thousands of flames fighting
    the wind
during a candlelight vigil in San Francisco in 1985.
Each 3' by 6'
tells a story, with a tragic ending;
more than a number, it leaves behind
testaments of lives terminated by ignorance and hate.
Applique, fabric painting, patchwork, collage, spray
    paint, embroidery and needlepoint, clothing,
    jewelry, human hair, car keys, stuffed animals…
Living through the '80s,
a survivor in 2018,

I have seen individual pieces, some belonging to
          friends,
could not bear to see more.

By purpose, the quilt
records
commemorates
honors
remembers.

The panel travels, leaves a trace of light,
yet a band-aid over a planet's still open wound.

I still wear my red ribbon
painted with HIV positive blood.
The fight continues…
One day I will see it all.

And to those I will leave behind,
all who left before me,
all those dear to me,
all those who have survived me,
I leave the design. These poems and you in them.
For you are my piece.

ABOUT PEARLSONG PRESS

Pearlsong Press is an independent publishing company dedicated to providing books and resources that entertain while expanding perspectives on the self and the world. The company was founded by psychologist Peggy Elam, Ph.D.

FICTION

Violet Crown—fantasy adventure by K.C. Littleton
If We Were Snowflakes—YA novel by Barbara D'Souza
Heretics: A Love Story & *The Singing of Swans*—
novels about the divine feminine by Mary Saracino
Judith—an historical novel by Leslie Moïse
Fatropolis—paranormal adventure by Tracey L. Thompson
The Falstaff Vampire Files, Bride of the Living Dead, Larger Than Death, Large Target, At Large & *A Ton of Trouble*—
paranormal adventure, romantic comedy & Josephine
Fuller mysteries by Lynne Murray
The Season of Lost Children—a novel by Karen Blomain
Fallen Embers & *Blowing Embers*—paranormal romance
by Lauri J Owen
The Program & *The Fat Lady Sings*—suspense & YA novels
by Charlie Lovett
Syd Arthur—a novel by Ellen Frankel
Measure By Measure—a romantic romp with the fabulously
fat by Rebecca Fox & William Sherman
FatLand & *FatLand: The Early Days*—by Frannie Zellman

ROMANCE NOVELS & SHORT STORIES FEATURING BIG BEAUTIFUL HEROINES
by Pat Ballard, the Queen of Rubenesque Romances:
Once Upon Another Time | *Adam & Evelyn* | *ASAP Nanny*
| *Dangerous Love* | *The Best Man* | *Abigail's Revenge*
Dangerous Curves Ahead: Short Stories | *Wanted: One Groom*
Nobody's Perfect | *His Brother's Child* | *A Worthy Heir*

by Rebecca Brock—*The Giving Season*
& by Judy Bagshaw—*Kiss Me, Nate!* & *At Long Last, Love*

Nonfiction

Other Nations: An Animal Journal—poetry by Maria Famà

Soul Mothers' Wisdom: Seven Insights for the Single Mother
by Bette J. Freedson

Acceptable Prejudice? Fat, Rhetoric & Social Justice &
Talking Fat: Health vs. Persuasion in the War on Our Bodies
by Lonie McMichael, Ph.D.

Hiking the Pack Line: Moving from Grief to a Joyful Life
by Bonnie Shapbell

A Life Interrupted: Living with Brain Injury—
poetry by Louise Mathewson

ExtraOrdinary: An End of Life Story Without End—
memoir by Michele Tamaren & Michael Wittner

Love is the Thread: A Knitting Friendship by Leslie Moïse

Fat Poets Speak: Voices of the Fat Poets' Society & *Fat Poets
Speak 2: Living and Loving Fatly*—Frannie Zellman, Ed.

10 Steps to Loving Your Body (No Matter What Size You Are)
by Pat Ballard

*Something to Think About: Reflections on Life, Family, Body
Image & Other Weighty Matters by the Queen of Rubenesque
Romances* by Pat Ballard

*Beyond Measure: A Memoir About Short Stature & Inner
Growth* by Ellen Frankel

*Taking Up Space: How Eating Well & Exercising Regularly
Changed My Life* by Pattie Thomas, Ph.D. with Carl
Wilkerson, M.B.A.

*Off Kilter: A Woman's Journey to Peace with Scoliosis,
Her Mother & Her Polish Heritage* by Linda C. Wisniewski

Unconventional Means: The Dream Down Under—
a spiritual travelogue by Anne Richardson Williams

Splendid Seniors: Great Lives, Great Deeds—
inspirational biographies by Jack Adler

www.ingramcontent.com/pod-product-compliance
Lightning Source LLC
Chambersburg PA
CBHW031135090426
42738CB00008B/1091